DUSK BIRD

Poems by

NICHOLAS BRADLEY

Cover drawings by Isaac Bradley

ISBN 978-1-291-35417-1

For Isaac
And In Memoriam Mary Bradley

*We must struggle to remain open - consciously to keep the chains
and blocks off the unconscious juke-box, so as to let its arm choose a
new tune.*

Nicholas Bradley, in a letter

*How do you know but ev'ry bird that cuts the airy way
Is an immense world of delight, clos'd by your senses five?*

William Blake

Design by Bill Berrett.

CONTENTS

THE J.C.B. OF LONELINESS

Lonely?
Tell me about it.

I am the excavator,
the J.C.B.

"That's enough," they say,

"you've dug enough
for that lonely road

going nowhere.
Stop."

I keep at it,
digging my own pit,

further and further,
dirtier and dirtier.

Some days
I'd like to stop

and swap a few
digging stories. There's

a man who can pick
a stone neatly

from a heap
with those giant iron claws.

He's always in his cab
turning on a threepenny bit.

Lonely, I call it.

LILY AND THE BROKEN EGGS

Everything will be made good

if not for you and me,
or our children;

every spark of right
goes on and on

printed like D.N.A.,
shining in its anti-virus,

coated like a shield
to feed on.

Each good deed
is a microbe of hope
in our star-pattern cells,

unknowable but felt.

We do not know ourselves,
or our crying out for help,

or our souls like broken shells
to mend.

AT OWEN'S FIELD, GOWER

People overflow my heart

and my tongue is just a stream
where they float like grace.

And in the swell not one drowns

but rises dripping,
into focus,
from the flowers flowing on.

I know they are going
and I have no power,

and nothing can hold their passing.

But their faces on stems,
like moons in my dreams,
rise up

from the current that takes them.

CLOUDS AT NIGHT

They don't last;
there are clouds like outstretched arms,

for seconds you can think
of order in the world

and patterns like hope,
or beyond words like that,

as soft smudgy forms
appear. Jots of prayers

that move on, clouds
of not knowing

what is what
with stars in between.

I've seen hand clouds,
backbones, shapes

that make you wonder,
changing fast.

SHEEP, NOVEMBER

Now that the cows have gone in
I shall miss them

and these sheep, chewing the last leaves
from the hawthorns,
are my only companions.

With their already grizzled faces
and strange tails hanging
and the thick bushels of their coats.

Still the pheasants ride
with ridiculous stiff pride above them,
obsolete and bottom-heavy,

while the sheep seem experienced
and masked
in carrying on their customs.

I feel green beside old hands.

TOMSY, PAT MURPHY'S BULL

"Jesus,what a pair of testicles!
Just wait till you see the rest of him."

He lumbered down the road,
a heavyweight boxer's awesome haunch,
his rumble slowing down cars.

They seemed so toyish, plastic,
wing-mirrors were their joke horns.

I walked behind him, an imposter
with a stick; one flick would have downed me.
Beside him I lacked definition.

I admired the phallus hairs,
the wonderful fur pattern of head and neck,
the piledriver brown hooves.

Then a heifer from nowhere,
a slim piebald, crossed his path;
for minutes he stalled at her scent.

Till Milly and Penny greeted him with a kiss,
eagerly following him down the fence.

CLIPPING SHEEP WITH RICHARD LANIGAN

"Now I'll show you how to knock a ewe,"
he said, clippers in his hand.
He bent her head round, felled her,
and lifted her forelegs back into his lap.

Black callouses were clipped to a mineral white,
hoods of foot-rot that curved around pus;
they were cut right back to a bleeding pad
to start again on the earth.

Then jabs against black-leg, dysentery,
a host of things, in a paraffin colour
entered their skin. And the smell hung round,
soused in our clothes, of sheep-neat, a reek of hooves.

How we wrestled them, writhing and kicking,
who could jump the gate in a flash.
They wriggled and heaved - "Ya bitches, ya whores!"
or lay breathing, beautiful, beautiful, between our knees.

THE RED HEIFER

I was mucking out in the barn
she was howling that high-pitched cow-howl
ripped up from sound-proofed walls;
her anus tightened and her stomach shook

at every tear. Being starved
to empty her bowels; the next day, Enniscorthy
would slit her life. Sun streamed in the barn
through early May's leaves' luminous green.

Something desperate edged her cries
as if the hook bit in already
and the iron line rolled along. Was it life
from the barn door, softening and mute,

as the afternoon grew dark for her?
Who were the jailors and the condemned?
"A stomach on legs," the vet said to me,
"that's where most of their problems stem."

MOOR MORNING

I step off
the green-hubbed Goodyear tyre

and lean on a wall.
The moor pours down

the back of my neck
and sprinkles my left ear

with a dull fervour,
a mute on its big voice.

Birds begin again,
little slips like thin goes

on a whistle;
a cockerel echoes

the late dawn's mist's
holding on.

Daisies still clasp themselves
like beautiful white acorns;

from the side
I see the pinkish, just-mixed

colour of their throats.

FROG BEHIND THE FRIDGE

Earlier, Isaac got the torch
trained on the shadow

behind the fridge. "It's there,"
he said, then went to bed.

I was reading my "Guide...."
but before I got to frogs

it came out
beside a pile of washing

and found the kitchen
interesting. I hardly looked

at its deep brown-green
and familiar crouch

of that pre-human epoch

as I put a cup
quickly over its head

and waltzed it to the back door.

The neat flip I'd planned

didn't work, but a quick scoop-

scramble did, and it was able
to view

the 2 a.m. back-yard puddles
at its leisure

from its all-in-one chair.

FROG ON THE ALLOTMENT

It was a good-sized frog.
As ever, that glistening motley

wash-leather skin - lemon, green,
yellow, black spots;

it went well with the garden leavings
piled up

with the rolled back old carpets,
April leaves, grass, roots in a heap,

it went under, blended in;

though watery,
its skin matched the land colours.

At first I saw it, after a spade-thrust,
spring up

then stop, elongate,
as if to show me itself

unchopped, whole, no missing limb;

as if I'd have a sense of it,
come from the beck,

and of where it fitted in.

ISAAC DRAWING

Like most kids' drawings

where it's all
all over the place

till you look

or the head's too big
and the body's wrong

till you see.

From tractors in perspective
perfect, at five,

you arrive at what's there;

and if people differ
they do
as it appears to you.

And sometimes you appear
round the corner of my eye

so small and tender
I am shocked.

If I could draw
you would be tall

as a tower in my life.

WINTER BUTTERFLIES

You have hung on the wall for weeks,
on unpainted bathroom plaster, damp and cold.

Your long offertory and deep meditation
see no end, but you seem pointed

as if to invisible stars; a clutched,
intent direction marks your sleep.

I have come to accept you,
the two that hang together

and the solitary dark wings, with a sense
of hosting something, a kind of pride.

As if I was chosen for what silently
goes on, an unspoken language

I might come to hear. Or just your trusting
to be still up there. I watch and wait.

DUSK BIRD, DECEMBER

I heard you, dusk bird,
singing down School Lane.

"Evening," said the woman
with her dog,

"Evening," I replied,
and you, dusk bird, seemed

younger than the hour
in your sharp chirp,

clearly lined, or else
you mark both ends

of the day with your words
I hear as:

"Drink out of bone china
if you can,

go for the best of your land,
not those micro-wave-friendly

Made-in-Korea
composites of who knows what."

I carry such a cup
with my flask; call me strange

as poets are, sometimes barred,
as they go about pecking up

bits of poems
like an odd exotic species

in their own backyard.

There might be scraps
of fat, a few nuts.

Honest, I find them odd
and I am one,

listening for songs
or making a bid
               to be that bird.

OCTOBER STARLINGS, PEN-Y-LYN

Like the fluttering giant pages
of a book,
the pouring shower-flick of wings

from the leaves in a whistling grace.

Cathedrals of the trees!

Organ stops once off their thinning lives,
this browning October,
autumn manoeuvres take place.

Sheaving, unsheaving, formats beyond us,
the birds go
shrinking their afternoon shoal;

they drain off our sky-space
and soak into trees.

Breathing ensemble, turncoat of wings,

see how their drift-swarm stops on itself
and soarers fade back
into their streaming sieves.

BEE, MID-APRIL

A bee with its fawn-fringed shin-guards
rests on the wall,

its joined wings' windbow shows
cursory lines
like arteries of zinc.

Yellow and black,
with its white rump's dark roots

while two glum headlamps
tar up front.

I saw it at the window
bounce against
this false clear world,

its section then slid out
to rub its bludgeoned head.

And on the sill, now dead,
its friend,
the fantastic current ended.

THE BIG ISSUE

I had to say:
"You've more money than me"

to the Big Issue seller.
"All right, mate," he said

to the poorest man in town.
I grit my teeth by sandwich shops,

make a detour, like the poor
I eat no chops. No dinner

in The White Swan but the woman
at the bar adds twenty p

to my fifty for a pot of tea
with hot water; that's four

cups better than the Kaff:
fifty five a beaker, and that's it.

The landlady comes to talk
about Stubbing Wharf, her life,

that there was jam sponge
the other day. She doesn't talk down

to the poorest man in town.

THE DARK ALLOTMENTS, EARLY APRIL

When I got there

I saw eight magpies on one plot,
one perched on a cane or a pole,

they let me get quite near;
it was raining, no-one else

around. I guess the wrens
and long ago hordes of small birds

are edged out. I half hate
these big survivors, half love

their beauty when I see them
close, by the four-foot pink

and off-pink bush; what is it?

I got digging, the odd whinny
of a horse was all this inner-city

garden had on its grey six-thirty
sound-track, as slowly the church

and houses on the hill
sank below street lights.

I had to get out.

TILLY AND THE PEACOCKS

I'd say it was the peacocks

with their strident
cut-through-everything
cries.

She was breathing
softly, confidentially,

leaning into me.
I had to hurry

where fennel
grew like green candyfloss
in May shadows.

Above us, in the trees,
two peacocks

blew all cockerels wide
and wilder,

KEEAUR! KEEAUR!
distress calls

to the usual bugles.

 "Call it Leafy Lane"
she said.

"Call me Flower."

LEADING MARIGOLD TO THE BULL

In a misty fluorescence,
a humid fade of rain

all day was tingling. Evening,
silver-willowed, damp umbellifers,

we went down the lane
with her wood-creak hooves
on tarmac.

How the sudden blare of her need
fog-horned the hedges,

beautiful, beautiful, it cried
release from suffering.

I wanted to lead all men
to women, all women to men,

where their blood blared
lonely, unheard,

and their breath warmed on the rope,
loosening at the gate.

Beautiful, beautiful, they wait.

SEPARATION, WHARFEDALE

I listened all night in a drowse
till the next deep trumpet

rose alongside; starting low often, then
ripping sleep open with a leap

to super-upset frenzy register.
How her head stretched up

to full length and her deep
cry-horn tensed along her whole

frame as haunches clenched in
and swollen udders shook

in one now soldered sore
birth-bag. Her calf in the shed

seven yards off, seemed to answer,
then not, in the night.

At five o'clock it came back
on. I heard the "Mind out!"

At the gate, "Get that dog off!"
"Patch!" Neurotic, highly strung

I felt pity for her sleep-killing
four-stomached bowel-wail

and her drum-tight unrelieved swell.

JILL AND THE PIGS

Before we pulled back the fence
they stood in the pen,
shifting their bulks, grunting,

moving their heads quickly
as if each time was a new idea.

Our dog went and kissed them
with the bond of animals
as if instinct told her

that the discs of their snouts
poked through the netting
for the last time.

Two boars for slaughter,
streaked with pink,
as if they had stayed up late and cried.

A bucket lured them to the trailer
and they went without trouble,

leaving a sparrow on the wire
rejoicing in its white breast.

IRISES, BACK ROUGH FARM

Although weeding parsley
I forgot the herb

faced with the weird purple armchairs
of irises,

the lolling tongues of deep sea creatures,
space visitors, their three-D

two-tone arms, tongues, and what
can you say of those velvet mobiles

entering your sense at a strange
angle in time and under-

standing in the rain where
you are never ready

for their invasion of beauty
and never could be.

PEONIES FROM HEAVEN

(Hollin Lane Allotments)

I don't blame them in a sense,
all of them; anyone in heaven

wants to help, to say Well Done!
They know how hard it is,

we're not here for long.
Many have grey hair.

It's not just somewhere
to hang out.

Lucifer and his missus, Swiss,
grow these gorgeous peonies.

We saw them as pent bulbs
before they threw their fantastically fine

carmine arms open.

I'd describe, if I could, how there
are rules even for these.

It's not easy to be one of them.

"It takes all sorts," the men
in flat caps

will say of an evening.
By that time the peonies

have thrown at least one of
their indescribably lovely shawls

back across their bodies of love.

RABBIT

Come for succour? I don't know,
ill;

the eyes are a blear flesh scar
and the ears like a flat refusal

as the sun strikes the grass,
from the hills down to the wet blades
blaze the tendrils.

Then a slow heaving,
the old weary and the head lifting,

opening like a wound from the throat,
a moment
to shake off flies.

When I see the mucus flaring
from those sockets' hollows

it seems horrible to let him live,

and his mouth opens in supplication
with a scarce, round,
ingoing whisper.

SWIFT

You just do it,

swooping under the arch
of a bridge,

up and over, round again
the ripe June bustle of trees

with the height of summer
on your insect run.

Again
a skirting purple
dips both feet briefly

in the stream
and out
like a skier on a roll of skill

re-judging how that paddle flits
and what instant insects

flicker on the tongue,
invisible as air.

SNAIL WATCH

The first I only glance at,
child, as you kneel

by the leopard shell,
antennae waving slightly.

Grey muscled membrane,
flange like a garment

glued to the leaf
and loose gelatinous throat sack

matching. It is mist stuck slow
and grey horn shellfish morning.

What I'd call the thread
of its neck, the whole,

is a slow adhesive tongue.

You rush in with a thrill:

"OH DAD! OH DAD! A BABY SNAIL"

On your hand
a tiny spiral, worm-like,
embryo or bait

close up, through microscope
of child, is grown

to snail. Untenable curl,
a soft dot put on dock leaf

miracle
of head and neck, a pin

slid out to sense the world
withdrawing from your finger.

CRABBING, ROBIN HOOD'S BAY

On the seaweed-wreathed
rock scars, shell-studded

the tide's out.

I turn back the blackish fronds
to see the ridged mother-of-pearl

stuck in the purpling
volcanic-looking bed,

itself like sea solidified
in moving wave levels.

He's searching pools

like children all over the place
with bamboo rods, green nets

on the end.

"I think the crab's motto
is 'hide'," Son says,

as he flips another stone
against the brown stippled lip

and hair-net of algae.

"I think you're right," I say,
as I wait on this rock.

(I'll come out
when everyone has gone.)

LETTER TO THEO

The work? I work so fast, sweat at the harvest.
Times, tobacco-dizzy, as the sun shrieks,
I fetch an emptiness, the limp head pounds.

Around they gather, whispering to disinfect,
the shadows that discuss me, posthumous.

But then, O heavens, it comes back
like sulphur to my tongue
the deity of day re-scored
and wild horse rollicking in blood.

Again the orchard shines
with apple-blossom, pure,
and morning, O sweet morning, breaking in my veins.

I see the spiders on their webs of breath
and feel my thumb-hold, whale's eye, pulse.

Step into life,
long grass and butterflies draw near;
I hear their murmur when the screaming stops.

LETTER FROM THE ARTS COUNCIL
TO VINCENT van GOGH

Dear Vincent,

Re -
your wish to train as an accountant;
first,you must get ten percent
of the fees out of thin air.
Partnership, we call it. Personal
costs - fuel, food, clothing, rent
are ineligible.
        Sorry,
that charming apartment in Arles
will have to go; and Gaugin,
who's no accountant
with that pony-tail and ear-ring.

Anyhow "your" house
will be sold when the car-park's
done. Can you sleep at the station
Free? Ask that nice Roulin.

(Thanks for the bedroom sketch.
Your hobby, spare time?)
        I suggest
you contact either myself
re- your draft application

or St Remy Asylum

        pp. W.E. Blog
        Human Resources Department
        (please quote reference number)

PUTTING SUBSOIL ON THE LANDFILL

In my clothes now is
the powerful souse, the sickly centre

we went to. Liam for the first time
felt the grease coat his lips.

Twenty years the rank blast
of this mass grave, this monolith

of filth, sitting on long-mouthed
toxins underground, like corpses

of fish, pressed-down bellows of stench.
As we shovelled soil and gasped

we saw the giant iron
torture wheels of a vehicle

tamping flat the foul hill
rising daily, as flies like locusts

clothed our van's cab in an instant.
Liam got out and took this photograph

of the burial mound, flocked with seagulls.

DESTINATION DUMP

Honest, Gloria,
living day in day out

with the rumble of lorries
going to the Dump. And the air

rotting slowly
and the stench hard to get rid of

and the rat dead in the oil drum
cows drink from.

All morning I wash the corpse-rot
out of society.

It comes here, Gloria,
next door.

I'd go out of my mind
if my senses let me,

if it wasn't
my job to stay.

SPRAYING 501

A vision slipping as I grasp -
arm up in the wind-drift vapouring the leaves.

Late September ; morning in a fine spray,
silica and horn, walking the fields.

How it rose,
hosanna, sunshine and air,
silking the night soil to the stars
over dung covered with gauze

and the toil of other creatures. Berries hung
their last, a claret-stopping taste
with a kick-back of rot. Apples

spotted, pitted, eaten by wasps,
furrowed their brown lips giving out sour.
As we turned back

a dandelion's lone ghost lit the lawn,
shivering and lost,
from the life-force that was gone.

BY THE AUTUMN WOOD

I go about, clearing up.
With heavy leather footprints

I avoid the webs,
there's too much beauty. I throw

teapot-warming hot water
in the nettles,

and see two spiders
in a large-scale opera

on top of
the dying green world.

I was invited not to spoil
their ozone layer,

their stage ropes' dewed frail
silver.

HAWTHORNS ON THE TRACK

Of what kind? Hardly a tree,
just above a shrub,

but proudly, stoically from its too old neck,
flinging all one way

with its bent aspect combed backwards,
prone,

waiting for the next blow of wind
to go with it.

So slant, so beggared,
spine angled to the land,

ligaments bent over, at the base exposed,
lashed one above the other

with spiky crooked limbs
up like survivors, or last flags,

but, like the sower,
protected at the bony core.

All this sinuous, spare,
where others like some gigantic cull of snakes
seized by the weather,

or agony of stags' throats
thrown backwards from the bole,

weigh back branches to flower
before the onslaught.

INTRAVENOUS DRIP STAND

I'm nearly off the drip
and my unwanted walking friend,

the tubular steel rod on five-star
castors,

sticking at doors,unwieldy turns,
forgetting, not part of...

this thin plastic feed coil
twists up,

"Intravenous Injection" tube
above the console

to the untouchable world
of the coffee machine;

one touch
for Columbian without sugar,

for a missile without tremor.

I'm
stuck in the opening two doors' gap

in the mixed toilets
with my surgical rocket-launcher.

ADMISSIONS, WARD 31, L.G.I.

Bed 11, with questions for the 65's
and over in a yellow folder.

I can't sleep with these two
plastic tubes in my wrist tops,

insulin pump, saline drip,
as if I was wired-up to write.

Gladys has gone quiet from her
Buggerman shrieks as Robert,

the ward orderly, cleaned her senile
smear. How she went on

calling ma ma ma
where are ya?

Now Charlie next door, 'confused',
loses his way through

the curtains, bursts in.
I stick my leg out to stop him,

point to the switch he needs
not his pyjama jacket,

to smother the light opposite.

ART

Now it's van Gogh's 'Vase
with Irises' he delivers
in gale force rain, wearing

a green P.O. top with a hood.
He's worried about trees

falling on us. I'm lifting
again and again these

corrugated sheets that the storm
blows off like wafers;

they flip, I fall, they slice
down the mud bank.

In the next lull I get one
back on, and a log,

then three fly together
backwards, sublimely,

as if the oak stop was nothing.
It's only temporary,

everything
is ripped apart and rained on

but a Degas pastel - 'Danseuse
au Repos' - stays where

the calendar and all else falls. Her
head bows toward

her splayed knees
as the postman hands me your postcard.

RUNNERS

The field thins;
we're out in front, or at the back,

but not the main pack.
What happened?

We still write sometimes,
old friends, since college,

less and less. A few get-togethers
a few less. Can't take drink.

Illness. Kids. Brass.
Thanks for asking

but so-and-so gets over-
bearing after a few days.

We won't stay.
And I'm left staring

at this page.

I don't do bad. I still get
more letters

than most
at long distance. See the ways

we slow down
or keep going grey like ghosts.

LOW

Coming back up from hell
is not easy, even if you've been

before; each time differs, save
your immune system is still

on low. I go to the library
and succumb at the virus table,

the rustle of germs turning the pages.
I go nowhere today, my face

is caked with the fake sugar icing
of Hades, Hypostop it's called,

'lemon' flavour, and it hardens
like the virtual icicles

of that place. I'm itchy and scaly
as my liver, once like a lily,

pumped out glaucagon below
while the gum-salve

was put on by Eurydice. Wow.
I mean a brown lily. Don't get ill.

SOLAR PANELS, DECEMBER

As always it was speaking
leaf-breath and branch-print,

this cold had it out.

Rapture, beyond it,
an ice-gauge on glass,

with the flash-bulb sun
at eight minutes

(All night I need a cloak
like this.)

Condensed chill clouds
daguerrotypes of dawn,

leave me vein and twig
in a slow adherence.

Outlines without blood
in their absence show

at the zero's first

Frost.

ONE OF THE GRIM REAPER'S MANY LIEUTENANTS
SPENT TOO LONG AT MY DOOR

When it's no longer just an illness
a week, or a month, off
and then on. When it's filled up

your organs, one by one,
and the pain gets hard to bear,
kidneys, lungs, and heart;

the lymph system sticking.
It's hard to know you won't
get well, but your sinking body

brings its own removal.
A deepening of that barrier
between you and it, an invitation

to a dream, with some neat
painkillers. On the road this week
I saw a buzzard hang above the flow,

holding there with its wings
rocking up and down, and feeling,
I imagine, some kind of bliss.

THE POND

I've got to go in the pond. Now.
Children are waiting. It's cold

and below is the gravelly, squelchy
mud. I'm talking about the pond

here, believe me, just that.
And that moment, shivering

before you dive in....and come
up....OK, and wondering

what that fuss was about, entering
the present, being now,

and the kids' beautiful bodies;
puberty, you can see so early

how it is, glistening, mud
forgotten, July as it should

be, straight in, no messing.
Go on, we're not here for long.

I'm not talking about the pond
now, well, I am, all the same.

Today it's warm, sun above,
cold below. Go under, then come up

tingling and shaking.
We won't notice if you're brave.

ERTY OP

Did you know that the whole
of POETRY is on the top row

of a typewriter? Alright,
there are numbers above that

but we're talking letters here
and this sublime line of the three

that make up our alphabet.

Did you know that Buslingthorpe
contains half the letters

exactly? I learned that
from Arthur Hopwood, local

historian, who gave a talk
on the Meanwood Valley,

and threw it in for good measure.
Thirteen letters. He's eighty,

if he's a day. As for POETRY
I found that out myself

or it found me.

SPARROWS AND OTHERS, MID-APRIL

Magpies follow one another
through the spare hedgerows
leaving impressions of a spread wing,
a frayed curve,
and the energy of their coupling.

The industry goes on; sparrows at their stonework,
feeding on invisible lichen
or preening in pools.

Under a seagull's shadow they go,
seeming no more of bone
than would sew up their feathers.

As crows take up twigs
with a dark muscular flap
forbidding their naked homes

and trees slowly clothe like creatures
in their own weight and essence.

Never were songs so sharp,
never were they so in evidence.

JACK-IN-THE-BOX

I won't stay down. I've had enough
of jails. Time and again I zing
up from failure, then the rough

lid slams. That's life, it's tough,
people want to jam my spring.
Just being is fine, but no proof

I'm here. So my roof
flips and I call out the hoardings:
"Come and hear my line!" And they stuff

me back in, keeping me like a Cruft's
dog or some other dumb thing.
They pet me, fondle my black tufts

of hair, like a toy in a trap. Puff!
I'm gone, as expected, no strings
attached; no come-back but a scuff

of hinges. Damn all those duff
shows, and bollocks to boxes! Boi-i-i-ng
me for once (alone on binges, chuffed

when I'm sprung) to sing off the cuff.

THE BILLY TRILOGY

1

WHEN BILLY LAUGHS

You can't help yourself
you fall into the wide silent total joy

that is his gift with white wrinkled lines,
you can't help it,

he puts so much into no sound at all
but a faint breath's blow

and laughter like a white switch
in his face.

So strong; imagine each line pulsing
with held-in, just unheard noise

on the other side.

There's a tape of him in the bath
left running like water, it is
with laughter;

the toothless warm anti-voice
is gone, the magnificent hollow

intense-as-a-shout absence
is filling. Hear.

II

ME AND BILLY GO TO THE BEACH

I'm carrying him down these wide steps,
past wooden handrails, to the beach.

His chair, left at the top, would have dug
into the sand off the ramp

if there'd been one. Billy would have
lifted the footplates up with his bony

white Howard Hughes hands without
the fingernails, and stepped into the sea

laughing quietly. As it is, we stagger
Death in Venice style without the music

over soft but cobbly sand. He kicks
a plastic Coca Cola bottle out of the way

and zips up the last metal notch
of his god-awful windcheater.

III

BILLY THE HEALER

You were there
so small in a way, an ageing

baby, legs stopped short
under the quilt. One tuft of hair

stood on your white grey head.

I spoke rubbish I'm sure
when the nurse came in

to your seventy year old Down's
Syndrome guise, who went puh-puh

blowing still faintly in sleep
puh-puh, wizened bellows.

Your eyes opened when we lifted
you up and she stuffed cushions

behind your pneumonia-waking
chest cough's cut

that alerted her. She said
we could not hang on to you -

your silent laughter, your white
grey shell ear, your beautiful

hands - if you had to go.

THE ANGEL OF RESPONSIBILITY

means thinning hair at the front
I'd like to think it's my hot brain,

not age, turning the rich dark
Amazon to a few sparse pines....

but is intelligence the thing,
of an odd kind? Or knowing

that there's less time to stop
and jot these lines down

as yeast is waiting to join flour
and a job application yawns

at the alarm clock I would
switch off. It's nagging me

always, this goblin on my shoulder
with strange access

to my inner ear that may be
musical; it calls on me,

whatever I'm doing, to listen
to the latest tune.

THE OLD STORE

I've lost something; the door
to my wit? CLOSED? Or soap for my step?
When I reach down

in a fix, the old store
is spent. Illness has crept
up, and really gone to town;

now nothing's on the shop floor.
Unsure, I keep going, ill-kept
by words that stumble round

in bags as I pour. More?
It's bad, though I've slept
off the worst. While the sound

stayed I had skill, like a vendor,
so each line leapt
to the till; through sense surround

of speech a sort of core
meaning shone. It's gone now, in debt,
in the market for new nouns

packaged and pressed. I've lost pounds.

NOT TO BE LIKE POETS

This girl I fancied, who made me wash,
just stuck me one on. Talking of an ex-con,
a suitcase full of self-inked dosh,

she said: "That's my kind of guy."
Poetry and yoghurt, I guess, don't belong
to winning women. They want money,

a house, security, somebody solid
and, hopefully, sexy. All this and a foreign
holiday. "Take me away! Bring me back to stolid

values, a roof over my head
and seven pensions. Give me the wrong
ideas about Art in which I'm not interested."

About the convict, I'd say, she's not serious,
but the money, I'd swear, is strong
for a shopping-mad Aquarius.

There are times, I know, not
to be like poets; to stop this song,
these books like faked wads of notes.

POEMS

You have to hit people over the head
these days to get your poems read, even then
you have to wait light-years till you're dead

or they get a new editor who's ahead
of his time, or hers, and will fend
off deciding till their desk bends or their bed

breaks from all that editing! Or they're fed
news by friends which will depend
on who's in and who's out, and who has said

this about that. Or who appeared on 'Drop Dead'
trendy programmes that wouldn't know one end
of a lyre from the other. Get wed

to money, grow your own food, instead
of writing. Take up the spade! Don't send
more poems away, sinking their lead

weights of paper, to fail, to bomb. They led
short unhappy lives among us like men
(refusals offend, as yet unposted)

and should on the whole be composted.

WITH THE SUB-EDITOR

Up in the air

I offered her one
of my ballooning poems

where the big 'Lambini'
crossed the moors

above Wadsworth, dropping
pink tickets with smaller

blue balloons. I could see
she wasn't keen. She chose

the dreamy bridge location
photos,
'symbolic' in her word

but for poems she wanted
no-nonsense language,

local interest, meat and potatoes,
one veg,

down to earth.

HOUDINI

I got out of that one,

no easy bout of chain-untangling
I tell you

it gets tricky when the clock
ticks

and there are minutes between you,
chains, a packing case

and oblivion.

You have to get a move on.

They dream up new locks, masked gadgets,
but they're all the same

in the end. One step at a time,
a knack of hands and brain.

Quick!

There's nothing like that click
of lock,

the rasp and slip as links let go,
unkink, and fall

like heavy clothes on the floor.

ENGLAND

England yobbed-up, pasty-faced,
blocked on concrete in the town square.

It's no accident you were born here
but it's wrong to think
of England as a land.

It's a dried-up limey column's
motorway of More.

What's "green and pleasant"
has got high wires around it.

England, you are stoned
on supermarket lager,
a barrel losing hoops,

no powder in your blown cask.

I ask you, do you hear,
you Empire of an old crone
whose heart is missing?

England, you are pissing
against the wall,

and England, you're our fault.

AUGUST SATURDAY, ROCHDALE CANAL

I saw thin lines like silver spit
come from the fishers
in meditation between the locks;

one had pulled in his long rod
so I could pass.

Their catching nets,
cigarettes, and huge tackle boxes
lined the canal. Lives were going on

and the silver-grey bream,
I saw two swerve in the clear,
were incidental;

a strange concentration was the haul.

It was male, a staring-out of water;
faces were set in a way I knew,
like a scowl as I crunched by.

Some were vacant and turned blankly
in that moment, then back
to the presences that would fill them.

THE TRANSIT OF VENUS

June 8th 2004, 6.19a.m.

So we were wrong, the Romans,
all of us, about Venus;

just a few fanciful poets

wanted a symbol, and doctors,
fond of Latin, wanted...'mons'.

It was good for Galileo in proving
we weren't at the centre

after all, but for loving?
How would it be

under an 'ocean' hot enough
to melt lead, with clouds

of sulphuric acid swirling
round...what's left of your head?

I'd like an easier life than love.

Yesterday was grim with its transit
across the Sun, the first seen

from Britain in 700 years,
an 'intense black dot' for six hours;

Venus on a hot spree, between
us and that unsayably strong glow.

Don't we know it, still today
stunned by the burns, the emotional
hits. It was awful. Venus is cruel.

Be warned of its transits,
all of you of the next century.

Maybe those in Shakespeare's time
were not so mad - as Edmund
jibed - to be on star-errands,

planet bets. We'll only have ourselves
to blame - if we want gush
from Venus, we'll get it

in groans. Big Thrush, two ovens full on.
I'd rather not roast there again.

I'm looking at the Moon, who,
as companion for love-ins,

did seem a cold indifferent
old pull; but now we, as we warm up,

the old Pierrot casts a shadow
that begins to look like discretion.

WINTER FUEL

I can't stir in the morning
but stagger in a slur of blood

slow November mist
sickness in a slab

tight inner midriff
insulin damage,

I walk in my thermal clothing
prickly T.B. beneath

King Wenceslas saw me
breathing deeply

ready to pass out
on Pecket track

carrying a blue empty
15kg Calor Gas bottle.

GOING OUT ON THE MOOR

Fifteenth freezing day
of December, gale's slant

axe blast can I
find the wagon's side

a place to crouch? There is no
shelter, just the need

daily. Finishing, my left hand's
polar bone claw

cannot wipe, so the right slowly
with paper and grass. My son's

next - when, where? Then the luck,
the stroke for my frozen hands -

a stone sticks from the bank;
prised out

it makes the perfect hole.
There.

R.I.P. POET

It's not good enough. Is it?
Being a poet. You can't make out

at minus one. You don't cut
a figure. It's just words.

Who wants them? Two a penny
is too much. It's not right

or proper. Girls will run
a mile from poseurs

who are "deep", and jokers
who are cheap. They want

strong sturdy guys who are
out of the house nailing down

dosh, tightening the screws,
while not afraid to show

their feminine side, but NOT
making such a DAILY BIG DEAL

of it in words.
Why not wear a skirt?

Get on with it. Hunt. Fish. Gather.
She'd rather have her father

back to pay the bills
than some namby with a quill.

It's not enough; no-one cares
if you write on water, air,

papyrus, stone. Get a chisel,
and carve on your tomb. Soon.

NICHOLAS BRADLEY

Photo by Christine Smith.

Nicholas Bradley was born in 1953. He graduated from Trinity and All Saints College, Leeds, in 1979, and then wrote a study of the poetry of R.S. Thomas for a Master's degree at Leeds University. But he chose to lead a nomadic life, working as a jobbing gardener and farm labourer in Yorkshire, Ireland and Wales. He often lived in home-made shacks, old caravans and tents. As a single parent, he brought up his son Isaac, two of whose early drawings are reproduced on the cover of this book. In spite of his poverty, privations and ill health (he was diabetic), he never wavered in his vocation to poetry. He died in August 2012, aged fifty nine.

ACKNOWLEDGEMENTS

Some of these poems, or earlier versions of them, have originally appeared in Calder Valley Organic Growers Newsletter, Common Ground, The Forward Book of Poetry, The Guardian, The Hebden Bridge Times and Poetry Ireland Review.

"Sparrows and Others, Mid-April" won equal First prize of £1000 in the W.W.F for Nature/The Guardian National Poetry Competition.

"The Transit of Venus" was included in the Art of Love exhibition in the Oxo Tower, London, February 2005.

"The Billy Trilogy" was nominated in The Best Single Published Poem of 2003 Category of the Forward Poetry Prizes, 2004.

"Winter Fuel" and "Going out on the Moor" are parts of a sequence called "Winter Piece" which won the B.B.C. Radio Three Poetry Competition run by the Verb. It was broadcast in January 2003.